The Long Arc of Grief

poems by

Laura Schulkind

Finishing Line Press
Georgetown, Kentucky

The Long Arc of Grief

ACKNOWLEDGMENTS

The Long Arc of Grief appeared in *OxMag*, May 2014.
Ozymandius Revisited, Speaking in Code and We Meteors appeared in *The
    Penmen Review,* August 2015.
Here I Weep appeared in *Poetry Expressed*, Spring 2016.
I Remember Her Now appeared in *Evening Street Press*, Autumn 2017.
Dirty Money appeared in *The Legal Studies Forum*, Vol. XLI, No. 1 & 2, 2017.
There is a Road appeared in *Light Journal*, Fall 2017.
The Sobranes Fire appeared in *Pennsylvania English*, Spring/Autumn 2017.
Death Rattle appeared in *Gold Man Review,* 2018.
The Pedicure appeared in *Origins*, October 2018.
The Art of Silence is forthcoming in *Third Wednesday,* Volume XII, No. 4,
    2019

Publisher: Leah Maines
Editor: Christen Kincaid
Cover Art: Lena Markley, Dovetail Design Studio,
        www.dovetaildesignstudio.com
Author Photo: Laura Schulkind
Cover Design: Elizabeth Maines McCleavy

Printed in the USA on acid-free paper.
Order online: www.finishinglinepress.com
        also available on amazon.com

Author inquiries and mail orders:
Finishing Line Press
P. O. Box 1626
Georgetown, Kentucky 40324
U. S. A.

Table of Contents

For my mother and father
Rima Schulkind, d. February 24, 2016
Herb Schulkind, d. July 8, 2017

Magical Thinking

The faded bed-curtain is tied back,
showing us the small adobe alcove where she slept—
her narrow bed, fitted wall-to-wall,
a woven coverlet, the colors of llamas.
Above, her wooden cross, her rosary.
Below, the tile floor worn from centuries of knees.

And on the bed, a pair of Levi's neatly pressed,
a small blanket wrapped in plastic,
bright white socks folded like snowballs.
All left, that through these worldly things,
worldly laws will be broken—
time, space, decay, the gravity that holds them to the bed.
Bits of wool and cotton made conduits for her healing touch.
Esperanza indesmayable, hope unfailing.

People file into the cool, darkened room,
cross themselves,
take pictures with their cell phones,
return to the bright heat of the courtyard.
I wonder if they are saving their photos to the Cloud,
and if so, how they reconcile what I cannot.

My mind goes to Johann Zahn—
inventing the camera an ocean away,
at the same point in time that
she walked these cloistered halls.
Reverent student of light,
even as he lived his own monastic life.

And Newton too—
devout as he formed the physical laws
that make sense of my world.

I cannot fathom it.
Even more, that Galileo—
father of science itself,
would see no paradox,
while I search his maps of the heavens,
and see no Heaven there.

Still, I cannot turn away.
The owners of these lifeless things,
somewhere surrendering to tubes and syringes,
while their hopes and miseries are here,
folded into each article resting on the bed,
absorbing its woolen scent.

Months later, Lena and I are drinking wine.
She laughs with her head thrown back, and
I think she sounds strong and upbeat.
Then she says she wants to go to Peru
to see her mother's birthplace, and
must see the worry in my face,
because she puts a reassuring hand on mine and
tells me she isn't planning on dying any time soon.

And yet, I suddenly remember the beatified
Sor Ana de los Ángeles Monteagudo,
her bed, the items left there,
the coolness of the darkened room,
hope and dust dancing a slow dance together in the dim light,
and find myself wishing
with all my heart, my heart, my heart
that I had something of Lena's then,
something to lay upon the bed.

For Jane

I.

This morning, a sparrow flew in.
A moment's misdirection,
an open door mistaken for sky.

She hit the bay window trying to escape,
fell stunned, terrified,
lay opening her beak in mute distress.

And I could not help but think of you,
even though you were right there,
already showing us how to save her—

lifting the cloth from the breakfast table,
bringing its sides together between your open hands
as gently as if the bird were already there in its folds,

while the rest of us hesitated.
So much life,
contained in so fragile a container.

But you would not do it yourself,
explained that you could not,
the signals from eye to brain to hand too slow.

What a thing, I thought,
to have the words
to explain one's damaged self.

II.

That afternoon, driving the Old Coast Road,
we stopped for a snake
basking in the caked and rutted tracks.

Whether frozen in fear,
or transfixed by the taste of our dust
on its flickering tongue, it did not move.

You stepped from the car and clapped your hands.
But instead of slithering off,
it turned toward you.

You stepped back in surprise, but did not waver.
No, you bent toward the shimmering coil
and clapped again,

insisting on saving her,
even though she wanted none of it.
And I think, it is not in you to do anything else.

Finally, she weaved her way to the side of the road
and up the steep bank, her long, striped body
a sudden mad zipper in the cracked earth.

III.

On our return, we went straight to
where we had laid the cloth
in the shade of the alders.

Relieved, we found it empty—
not a bone or feather.
No sign of a cruel end.

A day of small rescues, I thought.
But as dusk fell, and
we drank wine in the darkening room,

you began, calm and matter-of-fact,
in the voice I have imagined
you used with your patients.

How you had researched which subway stations were best—
where the trains come in the fastest,
the end would be swiftest.

And how you finally decided you could not.
Not for yourself, but for Jim who sits so still beside you.
For your daughters who need you.

And I understood for the first time
this greatest of rescues
as you slowly return to us.

Searching for Geronimo

I.

Geronimo disappeared while we sat
in a circle of mismatched chairs under the elm,
shucking the last of the summer corn
from your garden.

You peered up into the tree's leafy arms,
where he'd scrambled on sight of the visiting dog,
but there was no sign of the scrawny stray
you smuggled back from Mexico.

How long had it been?
I counted and peeled back the husks—
outer brown and brittle,
inner still green and pliant, pulled away

the silk from the surprise of neat white rows like baby's teeth,
even baby's breath, and said
I am "a-maized" you grow your own corn (ha ha)
and got you to smile.

By dusk, he had not returned.
You searched creek bank, barn, rambling house,
went into all the dark corners
holding out a spoon of cat food like a divining rod.

And I searched too,
hot attic, damp cellar,
for Geronimo,
for everything lost here.

Still fresh
to one rarely here,
wanting so to soothe what's past soothing,
to deny such hard healing can occur.

II.

Years earlier on another visit,
we sat at your kitchen table,
chipped coffee mugs—
me coffee, you gin,
my toddlers humming in the next room,
and you asked
from behind your dark-rimmed glasses
and the baritone that allowed you such questions,
why I had children.

I worried over my answer just a moment
before knowing I had to tell you the truth.
Even though I knew the pool where you found him
lay just out of sight, a few feet beyond the garden.
Even though I wanted to ask you
how you still slid into the water each morning,
or more to the point,
how you turned your head to breathe.
For the sheer pleasure of it, I said.

Just one breath,
and then you nodded,
approved the answer,
said no other could possibly make any sense.

III.

I remember this moment as I drift to sleep,
Geronimo still missing,
you in the next room,
the wide pine boards sighing
as you pace and call his name,
asking the ancient walls to give up this one secret.

My heart at once broken and healed,
healed and broken, by the cap capacity of yours

Ozymandias Revisited

Two towns in the California desert,
settled by those who settle deserts.
Those with nothing left to lose.
Those with everything to lose.
Squeezing hope from stone.
Digging, digging to the source of dreams.

In one, growers imagined palm fronds whispering at night.
Traveled to Arabia for seed.
Planted Deglet Noor and Medjool and Halawy and Thoory.
Called it Mecca.

In the other, homesteaders claimed their 160 acres of dust,
accepted the challenge to last five years.
Called it 29 Palms
for what was right there in front of them.

In the first,
came the cyclic pilgrimage of pickers
to this eastern edge of the Coachella Valley.
Some took root. Built homes, a school, a church.
But were treated like weeds.
Fought to stay on this dry earth,
surrounded by waste dumps and tumbleweed.
Hernandez, Arroyo, Benitez, Duarte.
Still, not many stay. The town swelling when
the date palms are heavy with fruit.

In the second,
they ranched and prospected.
Prudey, Bagley, Cambell, Bixby.
Built homes, a schoolhouse, a church.
Founded a clinic for soldiers after World War I—
the dry air good for their mustard-gassed lungs.
Perhaps from this came the town's discovery of
what grows best in that dry heat—soldiers.

They flourished.
Grew the biggest marine base in the U.S.
The town swells with young men.

A mural in the center of town
(on the side of the NAPA Auto Parts building)
presents: "Desert Storm Victory Parade & Homecoming."
In it, the marines of 29 Palms are returning from Iraq,
ancient mother of all date palms—
traced back to 4000 BC.
Another mural shows them toppling
a statue of Hussein.

These painted soldiers,
how many drifted over from Mecca,
from all our imaginary Meccas,
on a wind that smelled like change,
a few sweet dates in their pockets?

And what did they think
as their planes approached Arabia,
desert and date palms stretched before them,
knowing they came to kill?

And where are they now?
Do they drift with the harvest?
Do they cry out when heat lightning rips the sky?
Do they breathe the desert air and gasp?

There Is a Road

"Jane Crofut; The Crofut Farm; Grover's Corners; Sutton County; New Hampshire; United States of America; Continent of North America; Western Hemisphere; the Earth; the Solar System; the Universe; the Mind of God."
—*Thornton Wilder,* Our Town

There is a road,
on the outskirts of Arroyo Grande, California,
whose name makes me think of
the letter sent to Jane Crofut by her minister.

The name I won't say—
as it is after a father of ten,
whose living descendants still fill the Valley and beyond.
Suffice it to say, it is an ancient name,
a Portuguese name, carried
across the Atlantic from the Azores
over a century ago.
Suffice it to say, it could be the name of
a thousand roads.

I want to mail a letter there,
to any of the tidy homes,
arranged on groomed lawns,
with swings and flower beds and
hand-painted mailboxes, and
address it like this:

Occupant
"..." Road
Arroyo Grande, CA
Formerly a strawberry farm
Planted and harvested for 70 seasons
First by "..." and his wife, who arrived with nothing
Then their children and grandchildren
Until the bank took it over
And carved it up into lots
Taking everything
Even his name
For the road

See if the postman brings it, just the same.

The Soberanes Fire

Ash fell like a spring snow—
powdery flakes dusting the lawn furniture,
the windowsills, the vegetable garden.

The remains of mattresses and
kitchen tables and underwear.
All falling like snow.

This, our first sign of the fire
still two canyons away,
ravaging live oak dying of thirst,
bursting windows, melting metal.

Then came the blistered bay leaves,
carrying the smell of smoke,
floating down like crow feathers,
and landing in the grass.

Soon, we would start wetting down the roof,
turn to the inventory of our material lives,
pack the car as we
watched the ridgeline for smoke.

But, looking back,
the image I return to again and again isn't
the sudden orange glow
a hillside away.

It is standing on the back deck
in that snow globe moment,
catching flakes of ash in our hands,
as we marveled at how very far they had come.

Our sky, still clear and blue,
our grass still wet with dew.
The yellow warblers flitting in the alders, unperturbed.

The Long Arc of Grief

In the long arc of grief,
its end point beyond imagination,
I suddenly remember you—
how you stood at the corner of the buffet table,
one manicured hand resting on the white cloth—
and realize my miscalculation of your sorrow,
of so many things.
The hour of sunset, the pull of the moon,
the ebb and flow of the tide.

In the long arc of grief,
I no longer wonder how you tolerated the casseroles,
endured the Bundt cakes,
formed words.
How you put on lipstick, or shoes.
How you reached to find the clasp of your necklace
and survived the stillness of that moment.

In the long arc of grief,
I am not as I imagined—
all howl and hoof beats,
wild and furious,
clumps of hair in my fists.

I sip tea with milk,
ask if the salmon is fresh,
swim in the ocean,
watch the moon rise.

Each swallow,
Each breath,
Each arm outstretched,
Each rolling wave catching moonlight,
All in the long arc of grief.

Dirty Money

I.

Ninety percent of U.S. dollar bills carry a trace of cocaine.
Similar results worldwide.
From this, other inquiries—
bills tested for every illicit drug, every contaminant, every fear.
Heroin, morphine, crystal meth, PCP, amphetamines, nicotine,
bacteria, all there.

Telling us what?

Not that a lot of drugs are sold for a lot of cash,
or that nestled in tills,
bills rub against each other,
share their secrets. We hardly needed
science to tell us that.

News flash:
Dollar bills live a nomad's life,
touch rich and poor,
carry all of human joy, human suffering, there
in the paper and ink.

So why no test for these—
the *pentimenti*, the added value?
Below the dirt, the lucre, the fear,
hidden stories waiting for remembrance.

II.

Three times I smoothed and crisped the dollar bill,
three times slid it into the arrowed slot before
the machine accepted it, delivered
the soda I would not drink, but had risen to buy
to do something while I waited for them to tell me
what I already knew,
that I was losing this baby.

So many years later,
reading about ridiculous cocaine tests on dollar bills,
I remember this—
that it was three times,
that I watched the bill disappear.

And I imagine it now,
imprinted with the pain of that day,
folded in the dark of someone's wallet,
and suddenly long to have it back,
know I could love unconditionally
the one who has it,
if only he would bring it to me,
press it into my open palm.

I Remember Her Now

I would like to say
that I've thought of her often,
but that would be untrue.

In the beginning, after she stopped coming around,
I wondered about her.
Listened for her knock at the door.
Always after dark.
Her son hanging back, hunched into himself.

The first time, it was raining.
They were to be tossed from the motel that night.
The boy was hungry.
These were the facts of the matter.

She stood firm,
long neck, tiny straight frame,
and from the first she was my wounded bird.
I imagined her bones light and hollow,
her will fierce, her search for food endless.

I packed a grocery bag,
drove them back along dark, shiny streets,
paid the night,
tiptoed back in as if I'd been with a lover.

Again and again in those fragile months,
I would hope for her knock,
the flurry of filling bags
with what could be spared from the fridge,
scraping together cash for rent,
a nurse's aide uniform,
school supplies.

My memory is of them in our living room.
We sit on the edges of chairs,
cups of tea on our knees.
But, the room seems longer,
the light from the kitchen further away.
There is the quieting of dishes, the sound of listening.

And from the distance of memory
I see what I could not then—
how I worried over her
while you, my love,
quietly bent to the task of not dying.

What must have you thought?
Or did you know then what I realize only now,
as I suddenly long for her knock at the door
after so many years?

A bird to mend, a bird to mend,
when wounds beyond healing,
loss beyond letting go
are upon me.

The Art of Silence

The art of silence speaks to the soul...
—Marcel (Mangel) Marceau

He walks against the wind,
bent forward as he struggles
against the invisible force,
taking great, slow-running steps,
his painted face contorted with the strain of it.
Then suddenly, he arches backward—
the wind winning,
pushing him back, step-by-step as he
grasps futilely at the air,
until with all the strength he seems to have,
he leans into the wind once again, and
presses his way forward.

We laugh.
But, I cannot help wondering what wind he imagines
as he crafts the illusion.
Whether it smells of lupine and scrub pine.

Or as his hands become butterflies,
does he think of the white shimmer of the apollos
fluttering in the alpine clover?
And what of the invisible flowers
he picks with a flourish of his long, tapered fingers?
Are they edelweiss?

Does he conjure the mountains where he
created these silent gestures,
invented as a game to entertain the children,
to hush them, to give them silent play,
as he lead them, trip after trip,
across the Alps to safety?

And the shrinking box,
his flat hands pressing against
the imaginary walls
as they close in on all sides.
Does he imagine his father, the box car, the ovens?

I think he must.
Such gentle grace.
Such cavernous sadness.
Such comic relief.
These can only come from
love and loss and remembrance.

Speaking In Code

I.

My father could translate anything into Morse code.
As a child, I never considered why.
It is what fathers did.
And I would demand translation of the ridiculous—
Milk the fat cow. Cock-a-doodle-doo.
Anything to make him laugh, easy in himself.
That is what daughters did.
It would be years before I found his maps in the attic,
mildewed, frames broken.
Normandy to Berlin.

II.

I find my father's sketch pads
wedged behind his file cabinet, and
lay them out across the floor,
hoping he will accept the invitation.

Together we slowly flip the pages,
charcoal nudes mostly,
women and men in swift pencil strokes.
With each share a word or two
about balance or proportion,
yet not at all about balance or proportion.

We come to a quick sketch of a woman, a
few curved lines suggesting a backward glance.
He says he thinks this one has movement.
I say yes, it is very alive,
and mean I will miss you so.

He is unhurried,
for which I am grateful.
Another page.

He says he remembers the model.
I ask whether she was a student,
and mean, don't stop telling me your stories.

We open the smallest of the sketchbooks.
A sudden page of color and fruit.
He says it is a still life.
I say yes, it is a still life,
and mean, I regret not asking you more questions.

III.

He reaches out,
traces the softened lines with a
sweep of his hand,
and I remember how he could skip any stone.
And how I tested that.
Brought him impossible tasks.
Watched as he hefted my craggy finds
in the palm of his hand.
Then, he would lean his body into the throw,
and we would count together,
each priceless, weightless moment above the flow.

Here I Weep

We look straight ahead while I drive,
you next to me, curled into your coat
against the chill of summer.
You are always cold now.

I focus on my well-timed lane changes,
gentle stops,
smooth merges,
and think, I can do this.

I remember, years ago,
giving driving lessons to your first grandchild.
How, looking straight ahead,
we could share the passing world.

So, I test the "how to talk to teens" advice
that had served us well—
to do it in cars, where eyes naturally do not meet.
What else do I know to do?

Eyes on the road,
I try on my parent voice.
There are options to weigh,
steps to be taken.

You bristle. I try again.
Find a new voice for this unmapped moment.
I drive and ask questions,
and think, I will be fine.

But on the plane home,
I am lost.
No driver's illusions up here,
where all is surrender and faith.

We sit, looking straight ahead.
my row-mate and I.
Busy with laptops and crosswords and page-flipping.
A stranger, but still,
I hope he does not notice
I am weeping.

Home Coming

I can't believe you are here—
her first words to me,
the first day of the last days,
looking up from the bed that swallowed her.

Words I keep coming back to.
Couldn't believe I would come?
But where else would I be?
Where else could I be?
There was no choice in it.
No idea. No plan.

Her dying wakens my inner salmon,
inner homing pigeon, inner whale.
Coded to return here.
Brush, brush her hair.
Wet her lips.
Lie beside her and count her slowing breaths.

In the end as in the beginning,
she becomes my entire world, and
like a child, I imagine I am hers,
while she does what a mother does,
and lets go.

I Said Yes

She asked me
if I thought she would be dead
this time next week.
I said yes.

I knew this,
but did not know this.

How else could I have answered
as if she had asked whether I thought
it was going to rain?

I said yes, and yes again,
lengthening that moment between us.
One last blunt truth-telling.
One last intimacy.

The Pedicure

The first time I visited my mother
with my fingernails buffed and painted, she sneered.
Who are you?

It had become my guilty pleasure—
The soprano vibrato of the room.
The precise sequence of things.
Polishes like potions,
painted on with such slow and careful strokes,
clear then pink then crescent moons of white.
The lavender lotion, the warm towels.

Guilty, as I'd been raised otherwise,
sitting on a stool in my mother's studio.
The smell of damp clay.
The air warm if the kilns were firing.
I've never met an interesting woman with a good manicure,
a common pronouncement—
usually while wedging clay.
And we would roll our eyes,
the two of us against the world.

Toes were another thing.
Home sick as a child,
I was guaranteed every toe a
different color.
Bottles of reds and pinks and oranges,
spread out like little pots of sherbet.
My hand resting on top of hers,
while she stroked on the polish.

Her fingernails would remain defiantly
rough and unadorned.
But as her body turned against her,
she began to allow herself pedicures—
more and more flamboyant, her toes
bloomed magenta, violet, indigo.

And at the end,
after she stopped eating,
after the loss of speech,
her feet, shrunken like a Han madam's,
fitting easily in my hand,
I brushed on the Grape Pop,
Wild Wisteria, Purple with a Purpose,
toe by toe, stroke by stroke.

Death Rattle

The maracas, hung crisscross over your dresser
that on rainy days you would take down, and
let me play while you danced for me,
shaking your hips.

Your mother's silver rattle,
passed to me with stories of
Cossacks shaking floorboards
while she was born below.

Teeth in Russian winters; piano keys,
clacking, each time the baby grand was hoisted
into another Lower East Side tenement.

Sifting through your button box,
your strands of beads, your lipsticks.
And the urgent rattle of dice.
How we loved games of chance!

The click and chatter of pebbles
being pulled into the sea,
as we walked the cold surf,
arms locked, heads bent to each other.
Ice in gin and tonics on the patio.

Now, the week's pills,
being arranged in ice trays,
like a game of Mancala.
A bit of juice through a straw.
The oxygen machine.

I hear it all in your last breath,
your breath that I want to breathe in and hold,
until I cannot hold it anymore.

Her Porcelain Skin

I had forgotten her dreaming face,
her joyful and expectant face,
her peaceful face.

In her studio,
rolling porcelain petals,
joining them with a lick of her tongue,
building them into shapes so thin,
sunlight would wake them.

Her face before worry,
before anger at her own body,
before her long and ungentle going.

I had forgotten
until that first moment
after her last breath.

I thought I had prepared myself—
braced for the horror of her corpse.
But I did not know death would sweep away
the furrows and creases
that had become my mother's face.
I was not prepared for the beauty of that moment.
Her lips just parted.
Her skin smooth and translucent,
like porcelain catching sunlight.

d. February 24, 2016

I never liked the saying "right as rain."
What makes rain right?
Rain is rain.
It comes or it doesn't.
Sustains or destroys.
There is no room for human judgment.

But I had not imagined today,
a day when nothing is right
except this sudden, summer storm
in the middle of February—
torrential rain, lightning
hurricane winds.

Today I like the r's rolling off my tongue
like drops of water.
Warm to the hubris of finding rightness
in this cleansing, punishing rain.
The solace of a moment's fallacy:
The heavens, the heavens too, are weeping.

In the Garden

I finally made it back to the garden,
the one I planted under the alders by the creek,
and then let go—
back to the strangle of ivy,
back to thistle and hemlock and stinging nettle,
the survivors with their bitter roots.

There is little trace of my efforts now,
reminding me how I
first thought this place an untamed jungle—
hacking back the pampas grass and
woody manzanita,
digging up the German ivy by its purple roots,
until my spade hit a rock,
and then another, and another, in too neat a line.
How I brushed off each unburied stone,
uncovering a lost border of river rock,
and then a second tiered above it.
A double strand of great, gray pearls.

It was in these found beds that I first laid my garden.
Borders of pink impatiens, clusters of coral begonias.
But the transplants would not take.
It took me years to figure out why,
despite the spongy earth
under my feet, and
daily eruptions of dirt,
making manifest the animal industry
below the surface.

Years of trial and error—
More water, less water.
A bit more sun, a bit more shade.

Years of digging, of discoveries—
A glass jug (supporting the whispers of a still).
An alpine birdhouse.
A doll head.
A tea cup impossibly unchipped.
A bullet.

And in some spots a strata of shell,
marking the remains of a shell mound—
ancient cookfires and gardens,
dreams and tears under my feet.

Years of surrender—
to the indoors
to the necessary
to age
to grief
to the wildness of nature.

And yet, across uncertain ground,
like some decennial migration,
I am drawn back to what was and was and was the garden—
now an ivy mound,
and under the ivy,
bent ferns shouldering the weight, and
under the ferns, cool earth,
and a surprise of coral,
unfurling from dark, feathered leaves.

We Meteors

August nights we seek
dark meadows to lie entwined,
light show above us.

Still surprised each time
by the hush of these fireworks
arcing across sky.

Think not of their fire
but ours on this earthy bed
hurtling us through space.

August finds us here
beneath rain of stars, dying
in each other's arms.

By day, **Laura Schulkind** is a school law attorney, privileged to represent public schools, community colleges, and creative educational institutions throughout California. And, as unlikely as it may seem, lawyers (good ones at least) are by nature frustrated poets. They believe in the power of language, and think people's stories are worth telling. However, they are constrained to tell the stories of others; their own require another outlet. Laura finds hers in poetry and fiction.

This collection tells stories of grief-inspired and impelled by the loss of her parents, Herb and Rima. But just as they were her models for friendship, loyalty, and resilience, these poems move beyond her own grief to consider how we understand and support those we love in their grief, and ultimately how we all not merely carry on, but live.

Her chapbook, *Lost in Tall Grass* (Finishing Line Press), was released in May 2014. Her work has also appeared or is forthcoming in *Bluestem, Broad River Review, Caveat Lector, Crack the Spine, The DAP Project, Diverse Voices Quarterly, The Dos Passos Review, Eclipse, Evening Street Press, Forge, Gold Man Review, Good Men Project, Legal Studies Forum, Light Journal, The MacGuffin, Minetta Review, Mudlark, Origins Journal, OxMag, The Penmen Review, Pennsylvania English, Poetry Expressed, Reed Magazine, Reunion Journal, Schuylkill Valley Journal, Talking River, Third Wednesday, Tiger's Eye, Valparaiso Poetry Review, Voices de la Luna,* and *Willow Springs.* Her published work, and more musings on why "lawyer/poet" is not an oxymoron can be seen on her website: *www.lauraschulkind.com.*